# TERRORISM IN TURKEY

## BACKGROUND AND SHORT HISTORY

In order to put Turkish terrorism in perspective, it is necessary to draw attention to a few relevant facts about Turkey. As is known, Turkey is a sincere and devoted member of the democratic free world. One of the most important and distinctive peculiarities of Turkey is her Islamic religion.

Geographically, Turkey lies on the crossroad of two continents. She is a natural bridge between the East and the West and borders a region of differing political, economic, cultural and religious structures. This special location has made her the main target of the U.S.S.R. Additionally, neighboring countries have affected Turkey's national security.

For a country with a long history, the Turkish Republic is quite young. Following World War I, Turkey had overcome the threat of disintegration thanks to the resolve of the Turkish people. After the three-year war of independence, the new Turkish Republic was established by the Turkish people under Ataturk's leadership. This has been possible only through the full dedication of all Turks. In 1923 the Lausanne Treaty was signed and Turkey entered into the longest period of lasting peace in her history.[1] Major social and economic reforms were instituted between 1923 and 1938. These reforms were developed by Ataturk, the founder of the Turkish Republic, and were known as Kemalism. This ideological platform consists of six main principles which even today are a guide to all Turkish people and their government to follow to achieve their national objectives. These principles are:

- o Nationalism;

- o Secularism;

- o Republicanism;

o Popularism;

o Statism; and

o Revolutionism.

Kemalism is not a static idea, instead it is a dynamic way of thinking which can be adapted for all situations. Thanks to the applications of these principles, the social and economic structures of Turkey have changed radically. While doing this, Turkey has attached great importance to attaining and maintaining her economic and social development in peace and freedom.

Turkey's principal wishes are:

o To live in peace;

o To maintain good relations with all countries and especially with the neighbor countries;

o To respect the principles of independence and territorial integrity;

o Nonintervention in internal affairs; and

o Cooperation based on mutual interest.[2]

In this matter the traditional policy of Turkey based on Ataturk's famous dictum "Peace at home, Peace in the world" remains intact.

Yet, after World War II, the Soviet Union's historical demands on the Turkish Straits and some districts of Eastern Anatolia required Turkey to look for new arrangements for her security. For this reason Turkey joined NATO and Soviet demands ended in 1952. However, it is difficult to say the Soviet Union's historical demands have completely ended as long as Turkey shares its borders with the Soviet Union.

Turkey has been in the midst of rapid social and economic transformation in her recent history. The structure of the society has changed radically in the last 25 years. Beginning in the 1980's the state oriented economic model has undergone a change to a free market economic model. Agriculture is no longer the leading sector of the economy and has dropped below the ratio of industry in gross national product. Fifty-three percent of our population now lives in cities and towns. The rate of literacy rose from 48.8 percent in 1965 to 77.3 percent in 1985. The number of universities increased from 5 to 29 between 1965 and 1988 and the number of university students rose from 85,000 to nearly 504,000 in the same period.[3] Many social changes occurred and social demands sharply increased. These radical and quick changes in our social structure and way of life have created conditions such as shanty areas around the big cities, inadequate social service like road, water supply, social welfare--ideally suited to exploitation by forces both within and outside the country.

## THE ROOTS OF TERRORISM

As is known, the concept of terrorism is new but terrorism actions are as old as human history. During the 18th and 19th century terrorist actions were initiated by the Greek, Bulgarian and Armenian population against the Ottoman Empire. These actions were supported by the Russians, since the Ottoman Empire prevented the Russian expansion towards the warm seas. This tradition was left to the Russian people by the czar Peter at the end of the 17th century. This preoccupation with the thought of obtaining a warm water port is still alive today and needs to be kept in mind.

From the middle of 1960, Russian foreign policy has changed. Officially, they continued to show fastidious contempt for a gang of disorderly infantile leftists threatening the world's carefully balanced stability, unofficially, however, the Kremlim took an avuncular interest in terrorist "adventurers" of every alarming shade.[4] In this context, the Soviet Union's politburo decided to increase spending in the field of terrorism abroad by 1000 percent.[5] The student unrest that spread throughout the world in the late sixties also reached Turkey starting in university campuses as mild educational reform movements. The unrest rapidly changed character. Boycotting of classes, occupation of university buildings and offices escalated into violent clashes with the police and security forces. It is hardly necessary to point out that after the Tricontinental Conference in January 1966, student movements gained momentum and became political. A most important point is that these kinds of movements and student unrest previously had been seen in free, democratic western societies. The Tricontinental Conference declaration reminded proletarians everywhere of the need for close cohesion between the "socialist countries" (the Soviet kind) and "national liberation movements," providentially including "democratic workers and student movements" in capitalist Europe and North America. Its purpose was to devise "a global revolutionary strategy to counter the global strategy of American imperialism.[6]

Parallel to these developments, student movements in Turkey, which began with innocent student requirements turned into political movements which supported certain political circles. In 1970, the student violences spilled over the labor sector, when a Marxist Trade Union (DISK, the Revolutionary Trade Union Confederation) organized a strike in Istanbul which quickly turned into a violent riot and forced the government to proclaim martial law in that province. The object of this disruption was to destroy the nation's cohesion and raise doubts about democracy and the power of government among the people. There can be no doubt that, to some extent, demonstrations were successful. Political kidnappings and assassinations followed one after another in an ever-intensifying cycle of violence. Weapons made by the Soviets, such as Kalashnikov rifles were used. Consequently, the innocent student movements

4

turned into a worker's movement and after that armed struggle, in an attempt to change a Democratic regime into Marxist regime.

## IDEOLOGICAL INSPIRATION OF TERRORIST GROUPS

According to Donald J. Hanle there are three major groups and seven types of terrorism:

- o  Apolitical
    - oo  Psychotic
    - oo  Criminal
    - oo  Mystical
- o  State Terrorism
    - oo  Repression
    - oo  Military
    - oo  State-Sponsored
- o  Revolutionary Terrorism

Of these in the author's opinion, only military, state-sponsored and revolutionary terrorism are qualified as a form of war.[7] Regardless of the type, terrorism is generally based on violence to persons or property. Terrorist violence aims to transform the existent order into a certain model, under this model violence is divided into two as "left terror" or "right terror." The common point of the left and right terror is the opposition to the existence of a liberal-democratic order. Generally these two types of terrorism expend and broaden mutually in an action-reaction relationship. As mentioned earlier, the student movements in Turkey began in 1966. In 1969 these movements turned into political violence actions based upon the

Tricontinental Conference decisions made in 1966. The terrorist actions were
started by the leftists, more precisely, the Russians. Claire Sterling says:

> For invaluable clues in this case we are indebted to a
> defector from the KGB named Victor Sakharov, whose
> documented story is told in John Barron's. He was
> operating at the heart of the KGB's VIII department,
> embracing the Arab states, Afghanistan, Iran, Yugoslavia,
> Albania, Greece and Turkey. Accordingly, he was able to
> learn in detail about three major Soviet operations in his
> zone, they were:
> o  To sabotage Saudi Arabia's oil fields and if possible
> dislodge its pro-Western monarchy;
> o  To build terrorist cells in the Arab oil sheikhdoms
> around Kuwait and the Persian Gulf, notably Quatar,
> Bahrain and Oman offering scholarship and guerrilla
> training in the Soviet Union; and
> o  To mount a "brutal campaign of urban terrorism,
> kidnapping and assassination against Turkey.[8]

Of these three projects Turkey's was the most advanced by far.[9]

During 1968 and 1969 some promising young Turks were selected and sent for
training in Russia. After that, newly selected terrorist cadets wee sent
secretly for training to Syria. These cadets were trained in either Al Saika
camps in Syria, or G. Habbash's PFLP (the Popular Front for the Liberation of
Palestine), and armed and equipped with Soviet weapons and materials. This
returned to Turkey via different routes accelerated in the early 1970's.
Revolutionary-Youth (Dev-Genc) classic two-tiered form became a textbook model
for the decade's urban guerrilla movements.[10] An open political arm handled
revolutionary propaganda, demanding a Leninist regime in place of
parliamentary democracy. An underground military arm got going right on
schedule, with a "brutal campaign of urban terrorism, kidnapping and
assassination against Turkey."[11] There were several armed Clandestine
groups under the Dev-Genc organization. On account of the fact that the
terrorist activities had sharply increased, 12 March 1971 memorandum was given
to the government by the armed forces. Martial law was imposed in 1971 and

continued until 1973. During this phase, 5,000 leftists were arrested. By 11 April 1973 the police had seized 4,457 largely Soviet-made guns and 4,646,220 rounds of ammunition.[12] A non-partisan independent government was formed by the parliament. Everybody wished to restore and straighten out the democratic regime in the country.

## 1976-1980 PERIOD

After the 1973 general election, terrorism in Turkey entered into a different form. At the beginning of this period terrorism had spread all over the country and had formed different ideological terrorist groups such as at least 25 Marxist revolutionary groups, Maoists, Stalinist, Leninist, rightists, extreme religious, separatists. After the election a left of center political force set up a coalition government which soon proclaimed an amnesty. Most of those convicted of political terror and violence were released. These terrorists rapidly organized to start new groups. The terrorists had been continuing their political training and organizing, while they were in the jail. So, as soon as they released, they set up their groups. Moreover, the Palestinians had also worked assiduously inside Turkey under martial law to build up terrorist cadres. As Leila Khaled proudly announced to Hurriyet on 26 May 1971, the PFLP was sending instructors to Turkey in order to train Turkish youth in urban guerrilla fighting, kidnappings, plane hijacking and other matters--in view of the fact that it is more difficult than in the past for Turks to go and train in PFLP camps abroad. The PFLP has trained most of the detained Turkish underground members.[13]

The Marxists managed to penetrate the civil service and even the police force. After the 1977 elections no single party obtained a majority. Weak coalition governments followed one after another. Law and order declined to a

7

point of total breakdown. The excesses of the communist terror created a
backlash from the extreme right. Both leftist and rightist groups were
heavily armed and challenged each other in the streets, on the campuses and in
the cafes. The formation of so-called "liberation zones" in towns and cities
became a key goal for both left and right.[14] Left wing groups, including
the Turkish Peoples' Liberation Army, were aided and financed by the Soviet
Union.[15]

Huge consignments of Soviet-bloc arms were smuggled into Turkey from
Bulgaria, trucked overland or shipped by sea.[16] Meanwhile, rightist groups
received support from some rich Arabic countries. In 1979 the Palestine
Liberation Organization's spokesman in Teheran when Iran had fallen to
Ayatollah Khomeini said: "Turkey will be next."[17]

From the beginning of 1980 the Palestinians collaborated with Armenian
guerrillas and Kurdish insurgents in a common struggle against Turkey.[18]
The daily premeditated rate of killing increased sharply and reached 20-25
every day in early 1980. Consequently, Turkey reached the edge of civil war.
Between 1977 and 1980, Turkey suffered 5,769 killed and 19,305 wounded as a
result of terrorist violence.[19] Unfortunately, even in these circumstances,
democratic Western societies remained unconcerned until 12 September 1980 and
the Turkish military takeover. After that, interestingly Western societies
began talking about the human rights of the demonstrators. There is ample
evidence however, that the real aim of the terrorist campaign was not
primarily the advancement of human rights. On the contrary, the movement was
directed against not only political stability but also territorial integrity
and the future of Turkey.

The main cause of terrorism in Turkey was the outside involvement and
support which was directed by both the Soviet Union and her client countries.

The Turkish security forces confiscated 472,114 pistols, 3,095 automatic pistols, 30,183 infantry rifles, 4,361 automatic rifles, 13,636 shotguns for hunting, and 2,155,036 rounds of various ammunition in September 1980 through May 1981.[20] According to a report to the U.S. Senate:

> On 3 June 1977 Turkish security forces intercepted a Greek cargo vessel, Vasoula, on the Bosphorous coming from Varna, a port of Bulgaria. The vessel was carrying 67 tons of armaments allegedly destined for Ethiopia, contrary to the original information given to Istanbul port authorities. In 1976, Turkish security authorities captured Argentina-made firearms on some Turkish terrorists, it was learned later that these weapons were originally procured from Argentina by a Bulgarian state agency, shipped via air cargo to Bulgaria and delivered to Turkish terrorists all in a matter of a few weeks.[21]

In this context another impressive example had been given by President Evren. He pointed out in his speech in Konya on February 1981 that the total value of such a tremendous amount of arms and ammunition ran to 25 billion Tl. an equivalent of $250 million. He added that the total amount of money acquired through bank robberies and extortion by the terrorists do not even constitute one-fiftieth (2 percent) of the cost of armaments in the hands of terrorists. He asked, "Where does it come from if not from a rich external power?"[22]

## ARMENIAN TERRORISM

According to the historical report the so-called Armenian issue began in the latter part of the 19th century, at the end of the Ottoman-Russian War of 1877-1878. The Armenian terrorists of today are the successors of two of the most sanguinary terrorist organizations called the Hintchak and the Dashnakt which were set up in 1885 and 1890 respectively.[23] In order to understand the Armenian issue, it is necessary to know the 19th and 20th century of the Ottoman Empire. According to the historical records, Armenia was never established as an independent, sovereign state. Until the 11th century,

Armenians lived under the sovereignty of different empires. At the beginning of the 11th century the Turks conquered Eastern Anatolia, the Armenians were already under the oppression of the Byzantines and had, in fact, received the Turks as deliverers. The establishment and expansion of the Ottoman Empire, and particularly the destruction of Byzantium following Fatih Mehmet's conquest of Istanbul in 1453, brought a new era of religious, political, social, economic and cultural prosperity to the Armenians, as well as to the other non-Muslim and Muslim peoples of the new state.[24] However, Armenian propagandists in recent times have claimed that the Turks mistreated non-Muslims and in particular Armenians. Throughout history in order to provide support for their claims of "genocide" against the Ottoman Empire, since it would otherwise be difficult for them to explain how the Turks, who had lived side by side with the Armenians in peace for some 600 years, suddenly rose up to massacre them all. The Armenians, moreover, have tried to interpret Turkish rule in terms of a constant struggle between Christianity and Islam.[25] Essentially the problem was not between Turks and Armenians, but between Turks and Russians, because Russia had an historical aspiration to hold the Turkish straits and Eastern part of the Anatolia. At that time Ottoman Empire prevented this. The Russians had deceived the Armenians for years. Russian intentions to use the Armenians to annex Eastern Anatolia and not to create an independent Armenia was seen by what happened during World War I. The Armenians were left with nothing more than an empty dream.[26]

Today the Armenian claim has been based on great falsification that the Western world still believes. According to this false claim, 1.5 million Armenians were killed during their migration in 1915. As a matter of fact, the Armenian population in the Ottoman Empire never reached 1.5 million. There are various estimates between 1,056,000 and 2,560,000:

| | |
|---|---|
| The Patriarchate of Istanbul | 2,560,000 |
| The French Yellow Book | 1,555,000 |
| Encyclopedia Britannica | 1,500,000 |
| Constenson | 1,400,000 |
| Lynch | 1,345,000 |
| Official Ottoman Census Statistics in 1914 | 1,295,000 |
| Annual Register (London) | 1,056,000[27] |

In fact, it is very difficult to verify which number is correct. For example, in the 1910 edition of the Encyclopedia Britannica, the world Armenian population is given as 2.9 million and the Armenian population in Turkey as 1.5 million. It is very interesting that in the 1953 edition of the same work, the population of Armenians in Turkey is given as 2,500,550 for the same year. The article in the 1910 edition was written by a Briton and the article in the 1943 edition was written by an Armenian.[28]

As is known, the Ottoman Empire entered World War I on the side of Germany and Austria-Hungary against the Entente powers in 1914. Between November 1914 and May 1915 Armenian insurgents and terrorists caused many incidents all over the Ottoman Empire. As the Russian forces advanced into Ottoman territory in Eastern Anatolia, they were led by advanced units composed of volunteer Ottoman and Russian Armenians. Many of them also formed bandit forces with weapons and ammunition which they had for years been stocking in Armenian and missionary churches and schools, going on to raid Ottoman supply depots both to increase their own arms and to deny them to the Ottoman army as it moved to meet this massive Russian invasion.[29] On account of this fact, in April 1915 the Ottoman government was obliged to pass the Relocation Law, enabling it to remove the Armenians from vulnerable strategic points where they could assist the enemy.[30] Unfortunately even this law did not preclude the

Armenian rebellions and guerrilla activities. Owing to the shortage of men, most of whom were fighting at the various fronts against the external enemies, the Ottoman government entrusted the guarding of convoys of relocated Armenians to noncombatants. There is no evidence to show that the Ottoman government planned any massacres, although the relocation of the Armenians was well-planned in order to prevent further uprising. The removal of the Armenians from certain regions (six provinces) to others was a measure dictated by imperative military necessity.[31]

In fact, the Armenian population in Turkey in 1914 was approximately 1.3 million, the total number of Armenians who died during the war cannot be more than 300,000.[32] Yet, the 1918 edition of Encyclopedia Britannica said that 600,000 Armenians had been killed; in its 1968 edition this was raised to 1.5 million.[33] This figure increased with each passing year and in the 1980's it reached two million.[34] There were of course Armenians as well as Turks who lost their lives. The number of Turks who died during this period were more than two million.[35] Many of both communities died of cold, famine and disease and as a result of communal clashes upon the breakdown of law and order. Because Armenians collaborated with invading Russian armies, many also died during military operations.

Yet the most interesting aspect is that the politicians more than the historians are interested in this matter. These politicians generally believe in only the Armenian sources anyway. For example, the Turkish government opened the Ottoman archives especially concerning 19th century in 1988. Unfortunately no politicians or historians studied these documents. Maybe some certain circles are afraid of learning reality.

Throughout their 100-year history, Armenian terrorist groups have been indiscriminate in their targeting of victims.[36] Indeed, Armenian terrorism is an integral part of international terrorism. Between 1973 and 1987—a 15-year period—Armenian terrorists committed 199 incidents. As a result of these incidents 62 persons were killed and 380 persons wounded, and most of them were Turkish. Twenty-eight percent of these incidents (56) took place in France, 10 percent took place in both the United States of America and Switzerland. Armenian Secret Army for the Liberation of Armenia (ASALA) the Marxist-Leninist terrorist organization was responsible for 103 of the total 199 incidents.

Armenians are supported by some European countries. For example, ASALA's headquarters were established in Athens, Greece and Nicosia, Cyprus. As mentioned earlier, Armenian terrorists have been working in close cooperation with both the Turkish terrorists and Kurdish insurgents. Experts on international terrorism assert that the Armenian terrorists use proceeds from drug trafficking to fund their deadly enterprises. The deadliest of terrorist assassins, Carlos, recently proclaimed on Spanish television that his organization had entered into a working relationship with Armenian terrorists and was using drug trafficking to raise money to continue the struggle against imperialist forces.[37]

## KURDISH TERRORISM

The people of Turkey do not discriminate or identify each other as "Turks" or "Kurds." Racial, religious or ethnic discrimination is simply not a habit known to the Turkish people. Furthermore, from a legal point of view, under the provisions of the Lausanne Peace Treaty of 1923 (Article 37-45), there exist only religious, i.e., non-Muslim minorities in Turkey. The Lausanne Peace Treaty defines these non-Muslim minorities as Turkish citizens of the Armenian, Jewish, Greek origins. However, some circles are trying to artificially create a "Kurdish minority" question in Turkey. Unfortunately not only some Western states such as Sweden, Germany and Greece, but also the United States of America has been indirectly supporting this question.

In February 1988, the Turks complained that the U.S. State Department report referred to a Kurdish minority in Turkey, while also criticizing that state for the human right violations it had committed against it. This report was followed by what many Turks refer to as the "Schifter Blunder," for Richard Schifter, Assistant Secretary of State for Human Rights and Humanitarian Affairs. According to Turkish sources, Schifter "went out of his way . . . to prove that the Kurds were a different population from the Turks, linguistically and culturally," when he declared "we believe that although they (the Kurds) are not included in the Lausanne Treaty, they are a national minority by international standards."[38] According to the Turks, the visit of the Iraqi Kurdish leader, Celal Talabani, to Washington, D.C. in June 1988, seems to be yet another example of U.S. "hypocrisy."[39] Because it is hardly necessary to point out that the Iraqi Kurdish leader had been supporting the sanguinary terrorist organization, Partiya Karkaren Kurdistan (PKK), since 1988. Under the circumstances, the United States of America which is against international terrorism, supported these terrorist organizations which threaten the territorial integrity of Turkey.

The PKK terrorist organization was officially established on 27 November 1978, during a huge wave of terrorism. After 12 September 1980 most members of this terrorist organization escaped and gathered in Syria.[40] The members of this terrorist organization have been trained and equipped at the Palestinian Cephe Nidal camp and the Nayif Hawatmeh's Soviet-financed Democratic Front for the Liberation of Palestine (DFLP) also gave them excellent training facilities.[41]

The main tactic of the terrorist campaign of this organization has been hit-and-run raids on remote villages and hamlets. The goal is intimidation of defenseless people in an attempt to gain popular support. However, the people living in the region have categorically rejected collaboration with the PKK. The principal claim urged by this terrorist organization is that Eastern and Southeastern Anatolia were deliberately left undeveloped by the Turkish government. However, the Southeastern Anatolian Project (GAP Turkish acronym) is the most ambitious project that the Turkish state has ever launched and is a major economic step that will change the economic future of this region. As a matter of fact, this terrorist organization itself does not want the region to develop. This is the reason why the terrorist organization has been impeding the economic and social investments, in this context, they have sabotaged services the government attempts to provide to the region. Education, one of the most important services provided by the government, has been prevented by this terrorist organization through killing unprotected teachers and burning down schools.[42]

In brief, there are no political economic or any sort of systematic governmental policies of discrimination against the people of Eastern Turkey. However, certain terrorist groups based outside Turkey and supported by hostile circles are trying to exacerbate minor problems of economic nature which in reality are being successfully addressed by the Turkish government.

THE TERROR NETWORK

SOVIET UNION

After World War II, the Cold War era began and the world divided into two poles. Especially at the end of World War II, the Soviet Union became a dominant superpower, and by setting up an order in Bulgaria, Romania, Hungary,

Czechoslovakia, the Democratic Republic of Germany and Poland. She build the iron curtain between Western countries and herself. This was a kind of ideological war between capitalism and communism. In order to obtain world dominance, the Soviet Union spared no effort after World War II. Unfortunately democratic countries did not immediately understand Soviet intentions. The Soviet Union consistently promoted widespread revolutionary violence even while taking care to project the illusory image that the Soviet Union was abiding by the spirit of peaceful coexistence. Setting the tone for the r mission of the agency, Ponomarev (Boris Ponomarev, the head of the International Department of the Communist Party) declared in 1964:

> We understand our international duty as consisting of support for all the revolutionary democratic movements of modern times. . . . We, Soviet Communists call upon the fraternal parties and all the revolutionary forces to close their ranks more tightly, to overcome all difficulties, to rally under the banner of Marxism-Leninism in the name of the triumph of the working class.[43]

In this regard, the first signals were given in the 1961 Berlin crisis and in the 1962 Cuba crisis. At the end of these crises, the Soviet Union realized that she had to change her strategy to gain the world influence. As soon as Khrushchev was replaced by Brejnev in 1964, revolutionary export of the Soviet Union accelerated.

The secret services of all the Communist bloc countries were involved in recruiting spies infiltrating the world's nascent left-wing terrorist movements; special guerrilla training schools had been set up in Czechoslovakia, East Germany and Cuba for "selected terrorists from all over the world."[44] Many international fronts and institutions which were set up or controlled by the Soviet Union, such as Patrice Lumumba Friendship University, the World Peace Council and the World Federation of Trade Unions have served to spread Communism, especially to Third World countries. In this regard, the KGB and GRU tried to establish a number of terrorist movements or to take control of existing ones. There are many historic events to confirm the Soviet Union's involvement in international terrorism.

The most dramatic example of solidarity in Europe is the Bulgarian-KGB link to the Turkish terrorist who attempted to assassinate the Pope in 1981. The evidence though not conclusive as to Soviet intent, includes information from a Bulgarian official who defected in France in July 1981 and strongly confirms Soviet use of Bulgaria as an operational base against both Italy and Turkey.[45] Meanwhile, in recent years the phenomenon of transnational terrorism, supported by states such as Libya, Syria, Iran, Cuba, North Korea, the Soviet Union and the Eastern bloc. Terrorist organizations such as the PLO inspire speculation on the extent of foreign involvement in or support for terrorist activities in the United States of America.[46] In this connection the Director of the FBI, William H. Webster, stated that "there is no real evidence of Soviet-sponsored terrorism within the United States."[47] Yet, the Soviet Union is the center of the international terrorism. She was so in the past and is going to be so in the future. In other words, she is the mother of international terrorism.

## EASTERN EUROPEAN COUNTRIES

Democratic and open societies have suffered a lot of terrorist activities, especially in the 1970's. During this term, it is very interesting that as far as is known there were no terrorist activities in the Eastern European countries. The main and unique reason for this is the export of revolution of the Soviet Union. Of the six eastern European countries, especially, Bulgaria, Hungary, Czechoslovakia and East Germany have been involved directly and indirectly in these activities. It is estimated that the Soviet Union spent more than U.S. $200 million per year on training within the country.

17

The KGB also operated training camps in Eastern Europe. The most active were those in East Germany in the vicinity of Pankow and Finsterwalde; in Bulgaria at Varna; in Czechoslovakia at Karlovy Vary and Ostrava; and in Hungary near Lake Balaton.[48] If we take a quick look at the European map, we can easily understand why these countries are chosen as a terrorist activities base. If we compare the other Eastern European countries, these countries provide much ease to reach Western countries such as West Germany, Italy and Turkey. This is just because these satellite and client countries have been chosen to support terrorist activities in these countries. At the end of the 1980's many changes took place among these countries; however, there are many indications that the KGB still controls these countries' intelligence service. In this regard, the KGB was involved, either directly or through the dreaded East German security service, in the demonstrations that brought down the Honecker regime in the German Democratic Republic (GDR).[49] Christian Lochte, president of the Hamburg Security Service, said that "the GDR's spy network in the Federal Republic was still intact."[50] The same kind of situation also existed in Czechoslovakia. Not the least of Czechoslovakia's contributions to international terrorism was the manufacture and sale of semtex, the odorless and until recently undetectable explosive. The new president, playwright and ex-dissident, Vaclav Havel, revealed that his country's former Communist government had sent more than 1,000 tons of semtex to Libya—enough for 150 years of terrorism.[51]

Bulgaria, the most loyal follower of the Soviet Union, has used every opportunity especially against Turkey. Almost all weapons used by the terrorists in turkey had come from Bulgaria and probably other Soviet-bloc countries. The obvious example of this which was mentioned before is the Vasoulla occasion in 1977.

It is true that the Warsaw Pact (WP) disintegrated. Yet, we cannot say that Communism completely collapsed. Many radical changes have occurred in 1990 in both the Eastern European countries and the Soviet Union towards democratization. Everybody in the Western countries supports these kinds of changes. But what we shouldn't forget is the Soviet Union's doctrine and aspiration. In the long-term, there are no changes with her ends and means. She only changes her ways to reach global dominance. In the light of this fact client states and surrogates of the Soviet Union have changed their strategy to support their continued pursuit of world dominance.

## OTHER COUNTRIES

In addition to the Eastern European countries, many other countries such as Cuba, North Korea, Libya, and Syria have directly or indirectly been involved in international terrorism. Beginning in 1967-1969, terrorist training centers were established in North Korea, whose Communist regime was dominated by the Soviet Union and was dependent on Soviet military assistance. In that period Moscow was more intent on concealing its role that it is now, and the remoteness of North Korea originally helped maintain secrecy. The trainees eventually, however, have been traced to and in some cases apprehended in Latin America (Mexico, Brazil, Bolivia, Colombia), the Mideast and Asia (Sri Lanka, Malaya and Indonesia.)[52] Meanwhile in 1968, the Soviet Union made an agreement with both Cuba and the Palestinians. In two moves within as many months, the Russians connected with what would soon become the two magnetic poles of worldwide terrorism. So began their left-handed war on the West.[53] Cuba was especially involved on the West African coast and in Latin American countries. Castro had always wanted to export his revolution,[54] especially to the MPLA regime in Angola, the South African Communist Party (SACP) and its partner, the African National Congress (ANC)

19

and the FRELIMO regime in Mozambique.[55]  On the other hand, the most notorious terrorist organization, the PLO, has been trained, equipped and supported by the Soviet Union.  The Palestinian problem has created a more suitable environment, enabling the Soviet Union to assert control over not only the PLO, but also some Arabic countries such as Syria, Libya, Iraq, which fought against Israel.  As a matter of fact, the PLO and these countries have worked more in favor of international terrorism than to solve their problem with Israel.  By doing this, they have lost their credibility in the world and been with associated terrorist organization and countries.

For example, Syria still supported Kurdish terrorist against Turkey.  Also Iran has supported some fundamentalist groups in Turkey.  As is known, Turkey is the unique Muslim and at the same time secular country.  In this regard, especially Iran and conservative Arabic countries have selected Turkey as a target.  Intentionally or unintentionally, some Western countries provided some materials to countries such as Libya and Iraq to earn money.  For example, 207 firms belonging to 21 different countries, have provided poison gas and unconventional technologies to Iraq.[56]  Poison gas technologies have also been provided to Libya by some Western countries.

To fight against international terrorism is a serious matter.  All democratic countries should consider long-term benefits rather than short-term interest.  Because international terrorism is like a fire, in the long run, it will work against irresponsible countries.

## MEASURES TAKEN BY THE TURKISH GOVERNMENT

### POST-WORLD WAR I

At the end of World War I, the 600-year-old Ottoman Empire collapsed and had to sign the Mondros Armistice. Under the Mondros Armistice, the allies began to occupy selected parts of Turkey. According to the armistice the Ottoman Empire's armies were disbanded and disarmed. It was under these circumstances that the Turkish nation, under Mustafa Kemal's leadership, started the Turkish Independence Movement. In essence Kemal ranked the nation, the constituent assembly and the army in order of ascending importance for the successful execution of war, all organically linked in a sacred trinity.[57] Kemal noted: "First the constituent assembly then the army" and "The constituent assembly is not a theory; it is a truth. It is the nation which will create the army, but the constituent assembly acts in the name of the nation."[58]

At the end of the War of Independence (1922), the Treaty of Lausanne (24 July 1923) was signed. On 29 October 1923 the new, independent Turkish Republic was declared, built upon the ashes of the exhausted multinational Ottoman Empire. In the 20th century Turkey made her national choices in this context, towards modernization, social and economic development and a democratic way of life. Turkey has been aware of the fact that these objectives can be maintained only living in peace. Today the unchangeable policy of all Turkish governments is based on Ataturk's famous dictum "Peace at home, peace in the world."[59]

### POLITICAL MEASURES

Noteworthy political steps taken by Turkey include:

o Ataturk-Venizelos talks on 10 June 1930;

o Turkey becomes a member of the Nation's Association on 18 July 1932;

o   Balkan Pact established among Turkey-Romania-Greece-Yugoslavia on 3 February 1934;

o   Sadabat Pact established among Turkey-Iran-Iraq-Afghanistan on 8 July 1937; and

o   Friendship Agreement signed between Turkey and Greece on 27 April 1938.

Turkey followed a neutral foreign policy during World War II.  However, at the end of the war, Soviet Russia became a dominant military power in Europe and would not withdraw her troops from Eastern European countries.  The world was divided into two poles; the United States of America together with the Western European countries and the Soviet Russia together with the Eastern European countries.  The Cold War began.  Meanwhile, Soviet Russia, by repeating her historical request, demanded portions of Turkey, such as the Turkish Straits and three provinces of Eastern Anatolia.  Thereupon, Turkey sought her national security by allying with the United States of America and Western countries.  Finally, on 18 February 1952, Turkey became a member of NATO.  It is hardly necessary to point out that the Soviet demands did not begin with Communism; these requests has been continuing since the 17th century.  Soviet Russia has long desired warm water access through the Turkish straits.

At the beginning of the republican era, Turkey was a lesser developed country from various viewpoints:  education, industry, trade, infrastructure.  In 1950 Turkey moved to a multiparty democratic system and things started to change.  Although under Ataturk's principles there had been major reforms between 1923 and 1950, these were basically to bring Turkey into line with western societies to give Turkey a western outlook.[60]  Unfortunately, from 1950 until 1980 in the 30-year, multiparty period Turkish armed forces were obliged to intervene three times in 1960, in 1972, in 1980 respectively in order to rescue the nation's democratic order. Yet, it should be pointed out that the purposes of these interventions were not as reflected in some western media; to impede democratic rights or set up dictatorship. This measure was considered necessary to restore democracy. Turkey's army is not like other armies--Uruguay's or Chile's, for instance, or Spain's in the 1930's, or Greece in the 1960's. Twice before in the past 20 years, Turkish military leaders have kept their promise to restore civilian rule. They have said they are going to do so again, and, for all the fury of a frustrated terrorist underground, many or most Turks appear to believe them.[61]

After 1980's, Turkey fought against terrorism to protect her territorial integrity. Meanwhile the Turkish government has spared no effort to cut outside involvement in domestic terrorism. Politically, Turkey has always supported all movements against terrorism. Especially after the signing of the CFE treaty, the threat of military conflict has diminished in Europe. Yet, Turkish President Ozal said that "We need enhanced cooperation in combating terrorism, which threatens the fabric of democratic institutions."[62]

## ECONOMIC MEASURES

The Republic of Turkey was founded on the social and economic heritage of the Ottoman Empire. Especially in the first quarter of the 20th century, the economic problems of the empire had become worse. When the Turkish Republic was born on the scene of world history, she inherited only a heavy burden of debt and an economic structure that had collapsed completely. In this circumstance, the economic war of the Turkish Republic began. In the beginning, a generally liberal economic policy was implemented. With the scarce resources, Turkey had greatly developed prior to World War II. Although, Turkey did not actually enter World War II, during the war years, a major part of national resources was allocated to defense, which caused production to fall. External trade relations were cut and extraordinary measures were introduced. After the war, the scene was dominated by efforts to make a transition to multiparty politics and the arrival of military and economic foreign aid from the United States of America.

In the 1960's Turkey began to apply a state-oriented, planned economy. This continued until 1980, but there were political and social problems during the 1970's. In the face of negative developments that worsened towards the end of the 1970's and caused serious problems to emerge in the economy, a package of economic stability measures (which came to be known as the January 24 Decisions) was introduced on 24 January 1980.[63] After the 12 September 1980 military operation, domestic peace and security was obtained and a new constitution was drafted. This new constitution was accepted by 92 percent of the popular vote in 1982. And the new civil government which came to power after the 1983 general election, made a number of radical decisions in order to force the liberal-economic system towards a free market.

Generally speaking, Turkey was a traditionally agricultural country. As a matter of fact, Turkey is one of the world's seven self-sufficient nations in food production, with an exportable surplus. In 1981 Turkey's total exports were $4.7 billion, 47 percent agricultural and 48 percent industrial product. In 1988 Turkey's total exports reached $11.6 billion, while agricultural exports decreased 20 percent, industrial products increased 77 percent.[64] It should be pointed out that Turkey has certain problems in the field of economic structure, education, health and in various other sectors. Also, it is true that the main problem in Eastern and Southeastern Anatolia is the socioeconomic imbalance as compared with the other parts of Turkey. This is mainly due to the very harsh geographic characteristics of the region.

Especially in the last decade, the Turkish government has attached great importance to the development of this region. One of the best examples is the Southeastern Anatolian Project (SAP) this is a major economic step that will change the economic future of not only the region, but also all of Turkey. The SAP is a multipurpose and integrated development project, comprised of multipurpose and integrated development projects comprised of dams, hydroelectric power plants and irrigation facilities. It will affect agricultural, transportation, education, health, industry and other sectors. The SAP region comprises six provinces in southeastern Turkey, bordering Syria and Iraq, and covers almost 74,000 sq. km. of land which corresponds to 9.5 percent of the total area of Turkey. The region is equal to the total of the Netherlands and Belgium together. The SAP project is a combination of 13 major projects, it includes 21 dams and 17 hydroelectric power plants on the Euphrates, Tigris and their tributaries.[65] Eight of 13 major projects are under construction. All projects will be fully completed by the year 2001. The largest project of this irrigation and energy system is the Ataturk Dam and hydroelectric power plant, together with the Urfa Tunnels. Ataturk Dam, which is on the Euphrates, was completed at the end of August 1990, almost a year before its planned completion. This project will change not only the Southeastern region but also all the country. Turkey may become the breadbasket of the Middle East, as well as European countries.

Notwithstanding these developments, terrorists continue to provoke the people against the state, claiming that the Eastern and Southeastern region of Turkey and people living there are being ignored. Sabotage hinders services which the government tries to provide to the region. The most dangerous thing for the terrorist groups is the improvement of the region economically. No matter what the terrorist groups do, Turkey has advanced in this way within a short term. There is good reason to believe that this country will be able to solve almost all its problems.

## SOCIAL MEASURES

Turkey is the only Islamic member nation in CSCE, NATO, and the Council of Europe. She is, however, totally secular and free market. On 14 April 1987, Turkey applied to the EC for full membership. Unfortunately, the EC did not admit the Turkish application for full membership, saying that it would not be considered before 1993. In truth, the main reason for deferment is that Turkey is predominately Muslim.

From the beginning of the Republican era, Turkey has taken many measures to be a modern country. Generally speaking, Turks are patient and have common sense. Within the last three decades, this society had a great deal of experience with terrorism and with attitudes of countries including the United States of America. Turkey is a dynamic, young and energetic society. As a matter of fact, the main goal of Turkey at present is to integrate herself with Europe. This goal was set by our founder, Ataturk. Yet, this integration provides some advantages to Europe, as well as Turkey. For many reasons Turkey needs Europe and Europe needs Turkey as well. The last Gulf crisis and War of 1990-1991 demonstrated this reality.

Today, there are some non-Muslim minorities as Turkish citizens of the Armenian, Jewish and Greek origins in Turkey. Turkish nationalism is based on Ataturk's dictum "How happy one who says I am Turk." Yet, as in many other countries, some local dialects exist in Turkey. However, people speaking these dialects, which differ greatly from one locality to another, use Turkish as the common communication medium. Of Turkey's 57 million inhabitants, 47 percent live in rural areas. Rapid population flow from rural area to urban area has created many problems. In addition, annual birth rate is 2.4 percent in Turkey. There can be no doubt that a society which is growing and changing so rapidly will have social problems, such as unemployment, high inflation rate, housing shortages, etc. Yet, Turkey has covered a great distance especially during the last decade to solve these social problems. The resources of Turkey are limited; however, the needs of society are unlimited. Some social problems in Turkey will take time to solve. Yet, Turkey will become like a modern Western society in the near future.

## MILITARY MEASURES

Historical, geographical, political and national objectives are the basic determinants of any country's security policy. Events after World War II also played an important role in the formulation of Turkey's security policy. Geographically, Turkey is the natural bridge to Europe, Asia and Middle East. Politically, Turkey is the only Muslim country which is a member of NATO, CSCE, Council of Europe and associate member of EC. Turkey's security policy is based on the following objectives:

o To preserve and protect the independence and unity of the nation, the indivisibility of the country and the republic;

o To contribute to the lessening of international tension and to just and lasting peace in freedom;

o To prevent, with credible deterrence, the threat to use, or use of force; and

o To benefit from collective security systems.[66]

After the signing of the CFE Agreement, the possibility of war was reduced especially in Central Europe. To some extent the WP has disintegrated. Yet, the Soviet Union is still a military superpower with the capacity to defeat all European countries in NATO. Turkey has a 610 kilometer common border in the Northeast with Soviet Russia. Turkey also controls the Turkish Straits which connect the Black Sea with the Mediterranean. The defense of the Turkish Straits is vital both for Turkey and the Alliance. This is a major reason why Turkey has maintained the second largest army in NATO. The Turkish Army has many peculiarities. First, the Turkish Army strictly follows and protects Ataturk principles. Second, the Turkish Army believes that Democracy is the form of government most suitable to human nature. The Turkish nation also made an effort to strengthen its army against the internal and external enemy. After the establishing the Defense Industry Undersecretariat in 1986, the Turkish defense industry has been able to modernize rapidly to reinforce the Turkish Army. There are many projects, including the F16 warplane, armored combat vehicles, etc., operating or under construction.[67] These initiatives will allow the Turkish Army to become a stabilizing force not only in its own country but also in the entire region.

According to the Turkish constitution, the Council of Ministers may declare a state of emergency under Article 120 or martial law under Article 122. Especially after the 1980's, the Turkish government reinforced the police and the gendarme paramilitary forces to fight against to the terrorist groups. In this regard some legislative steps have been taken by the government. In addition, some special equipment have been provided to these forces. By doing this, the main purpose of the Turkish government is to keep the Turkish Army away from this kind of issue. In democratic societies, the involvement of the armed services in counterterrorist action is generally not approved. Yet, in some conditions, the armed services will be able to be used to protect the country's territorial integrity against terrorism. It is well known that the British Army is being used against the IRA in Northern Ireland. This issue is their internal problem. Few challenge this notion. Yet, if military force is used domestically by other countries, especially non-Western countries, there is inevitably talk of human rights violations. The reality must be recognized that human rights do not belong to some countries alone. Most are aware of the importance of this issue. The essential thing is to show respect for the integrity of the countries and not involved in the internal problems of the countries.

## CONCLUSION

There can be no doubt that one can find many definitions of terrorism. Almost all terrorist activities have common points:

o They must be planned;

o They must have been a political goal; and

o They must be based on criminal violence.

Whatever the political goals, terrorist activities share these common points and perhaps others. International terrorism has had a particular influence on democratic societies for the last two decades. It is not easy to find solutions to problems caused by international terrorism. Effective action is lacking because of our inability to agree upon definitions and to decide exactly where the causes lie. For example, we cannot reach a consensus on who is a freedom fighter and who is a terrorist. In other words, some groups are called freedom fighter by some countries, at the same time these groups are called terrorist by other countries. This is an interesting dilemma. Yet, at least, we should recognize that international terrorism is a serious danger which threatens all countries. To some extent, almost all countries, both democratic and communist, know this reality. In this regard, there are many promising developments between the United States of America and the U.S.S.R. In any case, in the short-term, the effectiveness of this cooperation will be seen, in terms of the fight against international terrorism. Yet, it is not enough for some countries to explain their determination against international terrorism. All countries must fight against state-sponsored terrorism. Some effective measures should be taken against those countries which support terrorism. Real cooperation is needed in the following areas:

o Intelligence;

o Training;

o Equipment; and

o Common enforcement action.

Turkey has consistently shown her determination to fight against international terrorism. Effective measures should be put into effect not after, but before international terrorism threatens democratic institutions. It should be obvious that a coordinated fight against international terrorism will only benefit world peace.